NATIONAL GEOGRAPHIC
School Publishing

Life Cycles
of Animals

Nisha Da Silva

PICTURE CREDITS

Cover, 1, 2, 6–7 (all), 8–9 (all), 10, 13 (above right), 14, 15 (right and above left), 17 (all sidebar pictures), 19 (below left), 20 (below right), 21 (all), Photolibrary.com; 4 (left and above right), 5 (above right), Jane Burton/Dorling Kindersley; 4 (below right), Ian M. Butterfield/Alamy; 5 (above left and below), 12, 18 (below left), Getty Images; 11 (above), 13 (below left), 16 (above left), 17 (above left), 20 (above), blickwinkel/Alamy; 11 (below), Roger De La Harpe/Animals Animals – Earth Scenes; 13 (above left), 16 (below), David Hosking/Alamy; 13 (below right), 20 (below left), Peter Arnold, Inc./Alamy; 15 (below left), Breck P. Kent/Animals Animals – Earth Scenes; 17 (below left), Papilio/Alamy; 18 (above right), Manor Photography/Alamy; 19 (above), Reijo Juurinen/Naturbild/naturepl.com; 19 (below), APL/Corbis.

Produced through the worldwide resources of the National Geographic Society, John M. Fahey, Jr., President and Chief Executive Officer; Gilbert M. Grosvenor, Chairman of the Board; Nina D. Hoffman, Executive Vice President and President, Books and Education Publishing Group.

PREPARED BY NATIONAL GEOGRAPHIC SCHOOL PUBLISHING

Steve Mico, Executive Vice President and Publisher, Children's Books and Education Publishing Group; Marianne Hiland, Editor in Chief; Lynnette Brent, Executive Editor; Michael Murphy and Barbara Wood, Senior Editors; Nicole Rouse, Editor; Bea Jackson, Design Director; David Dumo, Art Director; Shanin Glenn, Designer; Margaret Sidlosky, Illustrations Director; Matt Wascavage, Manager of Publishing Services; Sean Philpotts, Production Manager.

MANUFACTURING AND QUALITY MANAGEMENT

Christopher A. Liedel, Chief Financial Officer; Phillip L. Schlosser, Vice President; Clifton M. Brown III, Director.

BOOK DEVELOPMENT

Ibis for Kids Australia Pty Limited.

Published by the National Geographic Society
1145 17th Street, N.W.
Washington, D.C. 20036-4688

Product No. 4W1005064

ISBN-13: 978-1-4263-5060-3
ISBN-10: 1-4263-5060-0

2010 2009 2008 2007 2006
1 2 3 4 5 6 7 8 9 10 11 12 13 14 15

Printed in China

Contents

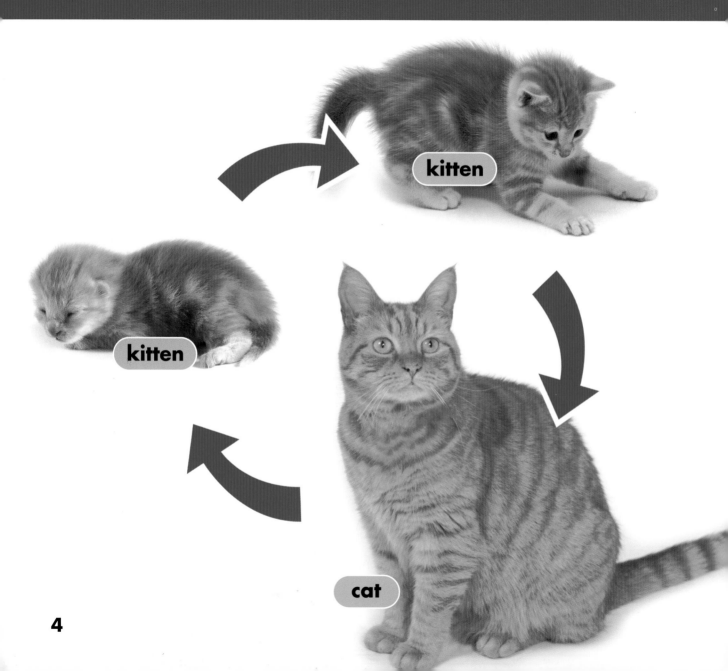

kitten

kitten

cat

4

Talk about the life cycles of these animals.
How do the animals grow and change?

chick

chick

chicken

Animal Groups

There are many different kinds of animals.
We can **classify** animals, or put them into groups.
The animals in each group are similar in many ways.
Their **life cycles** are similar, too.

Amphibians
Salamanders are **amphibians**.
Most amphibians have smooth skin.

Reptiles
Lizards are **reptiles**. Reptiles usually have scaly skin.

Mammals
Horses are **mammals**. All mammals have some hair.

Birds
Owls are **birds**. Birds have feathers, wings, and a beak.

8

Fish
Anthias are **fish**. Fish live in water and have gills to help them breathe.

Insects

Insects are another group of animals. Most insects have these features:
- six legs
- antennae
- wings
- three body parts
- a hard covering

Baby Animals

Different kinds of animals begin life in different ways. Most mammals give birth to live babies. Many fish and reptiles hatch from eggs.

A tiger is a mammal. When mammals are born, their parents take care of them.

After trout hatch, they hide to stay safe. Most fish are not taken care of by their parents.

Reptile eggs are soft and leathery. This baby crocodile has just hatched.

Birds hatch from eggs.
Amphibians hatch from eggs, too.

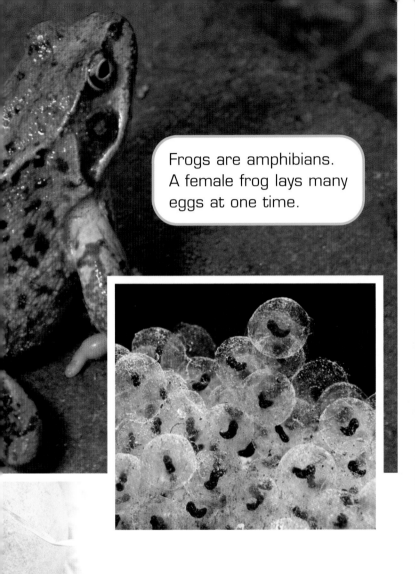

Frogs are amphibians. A female frog lays many eggs at one time.

These baby birds are Canada geese. When a baby bird is ready to hatch, it pecks at its eggshell with its beak.

Insect Eggs

Most insects lay eggs. The eggs come in many shapes and colors.

The monarch butterfly lays eggs on leaves. When the caterpillars hatch, they eat the eggshells.

Growing and Changing

Animals change as they grow. They get bigger and stronger. Some animals change color as they grow.

As baby mammals grow, they learn to take care of themselves. Young tigers learn to hunt for their own food.

Most reptiles shed their skin as they grow. This crocodile sheds one scale at a time.

As this Canada goose gets older, its feathers grow long and strong so it can fly.

A trout changes color as it grows.

Some animals go through very different stages as they grow. This process is called **metamorphosis**.

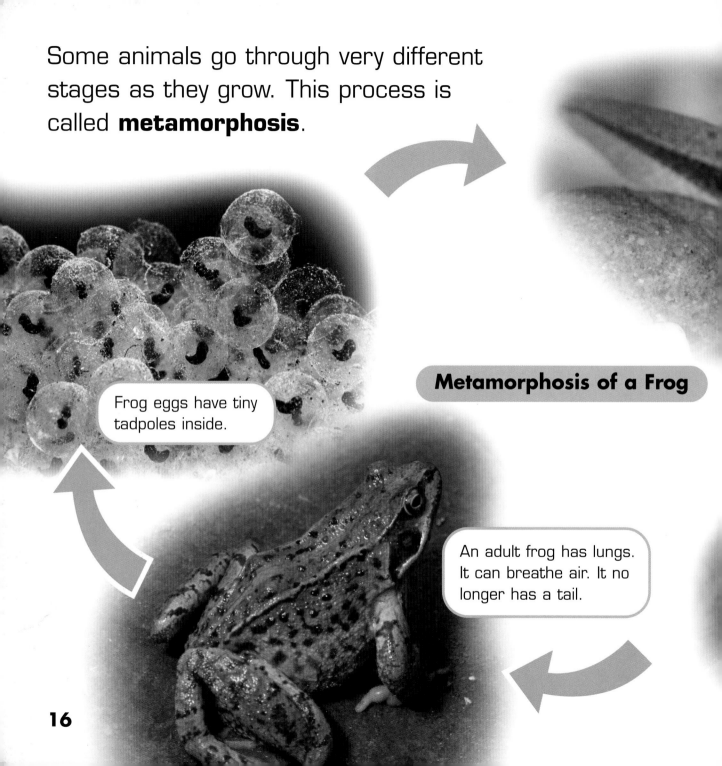

Metamorphosis of a Frog

Frog eggs have tiny tadpoles inside.

An adult frog has lungs. It can breathe air. It no longer has a tail.

A young tadpole has a tail. It uses gills to breathe in water.

As the tadpole gets older, it grows legs.

Insect Metamorphosis

Some insects go through metamorphosis, too. Look at the life cycle below. A butterfly goes from an egg, to a caterpillar, to a **chrysalis** before it becomes a butterfly.

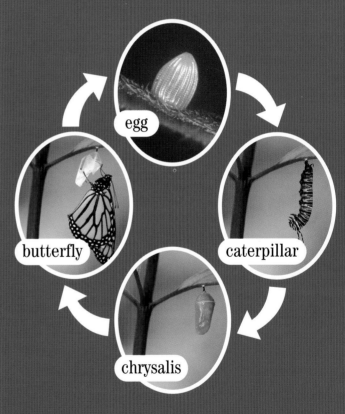

egg

caterpillar

chrysalis

butterfly

New Life

When a young animal becomes an adult, it is ready to find a mate and **reproduce**.

Female frogs usually lay their eggs in water.

A female tiger usually has two or three cubs.

Many birds sit on their eggs to keep them warm.

A female trout can lay up to 60 eggs. The male trout stays nearby.

This female crocodile covers her eggs with sand. The male crocodile keeps watch.

20

amphibian

bird

classify

fish

life cycle

mammal

metamorphosis

reproduce

reptile

21

Glossary

amphibian (page 6)
A kind of animal that has smooth skin and usually goes through metamorphosis as it grows
A salamander is a kind of amphibian.

bird (page 8)
A kind of animal that has feathers, wings, and a beak
An owl is a kind of bird.

chrysalis (page 17)
The shell that covers a caterpillar while it develops into a butterfly
A monarch caterpillar develops a chrysalis before it changes into a butterfly.

classify (page 6)
To sort things into groups with similar features
Scientists classify animals that have wings as birds.

fish (page 9)
A kind of animal that lives in water and usually has scales, fins, and gills
An anthia is a kind of fish.

life cycle (page 6)
The stages an animal goes through during its life
Reproduction is an important stage in animal life cycles.

mammal (page 7)
A kind of animal that has hair and produces milk for its young
A horse is a kind of mammal.

metamorphosis (page 16)
To change form as part of growth
A tadpole goes through metamorphosis to become a frog.

reproduce (page 18)
To make new life
When animals reproduce, they have babies.

reptile (page 7)
A kind of animal that has scaly skin and usually lays eggs
An iguana is a kind of reptile.

Index